COLLEGE
CATS

Also available from HarperCollinsPublishers
by Richard Surman

CATHEDRAL CATS

COLLEGE
CATS

Richard Surman

HarperCollins*Publishers*

HarperCollins*Publishers*
77-85 Fulham Palace Road, London W6 8JB

First published in Great Britain
in 1994 by HarperCollins*Publishers*

1 3 5 7 9 10 8 6 4 2

Copyright © 1994 Richard Surman

Richard Surman asserts the moral right to be
identified as the author and photographer of this work

A catalogue record for this book is
available from the British Library

0 00 627869-8

Printed and bound by
HarperCollins*Manufacturing*, Hong Kong

For Gabriel, Carlos, Luke and Joby

Contents

Introduction

The cats of Oxford and Cambridge colleges are neighbours. They trespass on each other's territories, visit people in other colleges, and above all, fight inter-collegiate battles. Bastions of academic excellence, rich in historic and architectural interest and in many cases welcome havens of eccentricity – the colleges offer another irresistible opportunity to find characterful cats.

When I started to research the book, I had no particular concerns about finding cats – I knew they'd be there. They were, sometimes in startlingly large numbers – bold, dominating, shy, strange, funny, peculiar, intelligent or dozy. Burbage at Trinity tried to climb up the chimney at the sight of a camera. Diplock at Worcester led me through twenty-six acres of garden, only ever stopping to evaluate his chances of catching a squirrel. Oriel's Polly Flinders patiently allowed herself to be walked through an archway again and again, whilst Bossuet at Caius scampered madly around Tree Court. Olga noisily but patiently put up with our attempts to induce her to sit on a windowsill. Jessica was brought back to Westcott under protest from her favourite bookshop.

My own passion for cats was inherited from my family, in particular my father, with whom cats occupied ridiculously pampered positions. Even the really badly behaved ones, like Winnie, my sister Jane's cat, who sank her teeth into all and sundry, were treated like convalescent royalty. I'm convinced that my father never actually got any work done in his study, because whenever I saw him he was gently shooing one of a number of fabulously idle cats who were flopped over the desk, or he was perching on the edge of his chair to avoid disturbing an inert lump of tabby. Even a disaster in the wine cellar couldn't dampen his lenient attitude towards cats. They'd always make it to the beds before us, and we'd have to contort ourselves around some stubbornly sleeping feline. Our cats also defied the laws of physics. When I tried to lift one off a bed or a chair, it could miraculously increase its mass without changing size.

Cats got away with so many things that I wanted to get away with and more besides. Ours stole food, woke everyone up at any hour of the night, took the best chairs and the most comfortable beds, dug up precious plants, dumped dead birds all over the house and ate Harriet the hampster. Why do they escape with impunity while children get caught? Now I think I know. They permit an illusion of ownership but no one truly owns, let alone controls, a cat. They tolerate us. The breeding makes no difference either. The cutest looking cat can be a raging demon at heart, whilst the most battered and scarred 'moggy' can be as soft as warm butter.

I am very grateful to my editor, Giles Semper, for his enthusiasm and support, and for giving me another opportunity to indulge my own affection for cats.

I would also like to thank particularly Dusha Bateson of King's College for her great help in researching illustrations, Dr Mika Oldham of Jesus College, Professor Anne Barton and Dr Hazel McLean of Trinity College, Cambridge for supplying me with background information, and all the many people who didn't have cats, but who helped me to track them down. I am very grateful to Tim and Alex Cotton, who made some invaluable contributions to my research, and provided me with a bicycle on which to wobble around Cambridge. I also wish to express my appreciation of my family's forbearance in the face of endless anecdotes about 'my' college cats. My final thanks go to Jingles, our temporarily resident Brown Burmese cat, who helped with the proof reading, whilst sitting in bed with me, eating toast and honey.

Kipper

Kipper is not a lucky cat.
Wherever she ventured in her new Cambridge
home, she was set upon by a new feline adversary.

At first Kipper seemed quite content in the family's temporary residence when Bob Hepple was appointed Master of Clare. Then one afternoon there was a terrible shrieking from the garden, and a startled Mary Coussey – Bob Hepple's wife – looked out of the window to see Kipper being brutalized by a gigantic tabby tomcat. Kipper dashed into the house, still pursued by this tartar of a cat.

It was a couple of days before she plucked up the courage to go out again. She was halfway down the garden, when the rapacious tabby exploded out of a shrub. Poor Kipper fled again, just managing to make it to the safety of the house. She decided that the house was her only sanctuary against this unprovoked aggression.

A few more days passed. Kipper was sitting at the top of the stairs washing when Mary Coussey opened the front door. Before anyone had time to react, the tabby dashed in, ran up the stairs, drove Kipper into a bedroom and attacked her even more ferociously than before. Mary Coussey drove him off, but by now Kipper's confidence had been shattered.

Kipper: alert for new feline incursions

Kipper had bided her time before moving into the family's former London home, waiting until everyone was away on holiday before quietly moving her litter of kittens from the garden to behind one of the children's beds. The cat seemed so happy that Mary Coussey let her stay. The children's nanny had named the cat 'Fish Face', which the children moderated to Kipper.

Kipper's permanent home forms part of an attractive courtyard, built in the seventeenth-century, replacing buildings that dated from the founding of the college in 1338 by Lady Elizabeth de Clare, a granddaughter of Edward I. After her terrible initiation to Cambridge, Kipper warily explored her new environment, making tentative forays into the Lodge garden which runs down to the river Cam. Little did she

A tentative garden stroll

Kipper makes sure the coast is clear

suspect that she was walking into another series of long-standing territorial disputes and overlapping feline rights of way. It needed the cat equivalent of a peacekeeping force. First came Titan from Trinity, landing in the garden with a thump, glaring at Kipper, and stalking over to deliver a good cuff round the head. A weary Kipper retreated to the safety of the Lodge, finding an apparently safe haven in the first floor drawing room.

However, she had reckoned without Caiaphas, cat to the Chaplain of St John's. It is not clear what he got up to, but Kipper was found one afternoon cowering in the corner of the kitchen and later Bob Hepple discovered a black and white cat curled up in a comfortable armchair in the drawing room. A glass of water was sufficient to dislodge a protesting Caiaphas thus ensuring that, at the very least, Kipper could enjoy some domestic peace.

Sprocket

Sprocket's first serious involvement in college affairs began with his housing advice column in FitzBits, the college magazine.

A serene Sprocket dreams up outrageous comments for his Fitzbits columns

His intimate knowledge of the accommodation made him a natural choice as writer. His popularity soared and he was nominated for Junior President. He spurned the hustings in favour of chasing a squirrel, but managed to achieve twelve votes. Then he made his crucial move to the lonely hearts desk of *FitzBits*. The opinions he expresses here are frankly outrageous, and may not be quoted in the interests of propriety. His frequent visits to the college chapel are probably for overdue acts of contrition, but they fool no one.

Sprocket defected to Fitzwilliam. Unknown to David Holton, the Building Superintendent, Sprocket already had a good home nearby. When it was discovered that he was leading a double life, he was regularly carried back home, only to reappear shortly afterwards.

One day his owners told David Holton that they had to move house. As Sprocket had become so attached to the college, they wondered if he might stay on as the official college cat. Sprocket probably had no intention of leaving anyway. Nowadays Sprocket's bank account is replenished from the first year discotheque. Freshers place their donations in a large bin, some making rather more extravagant donations than is perhaps wise.

At half past eleven in the morning Sprocket heads for the centre block, where he sits at the junction of the servery corridor and the corridor leading to the Junior Common Room bar. He is met by one of the

Sprocket's college chapel vantage point

Checking for open windows

serving ladies bearing a large plate of pork or chicken for his lunch.

Originally a non-collegiate society for poorer students, who were unable to pay the substantial fees required by other university colleges, Fitzwilliam House moved from its premises opposite the Fitzwilliam Museum, to its present site in Huntingdon Road. Fitzwilliam's architect Sir Denys Lasdun managed to translate the courtyard, cloister and common room features of traditional college architecture into a pleasing modern style – open, spacious, airy and accessible. In other words, it is perfect for a cat.

Nowhere is off limits for Sprocket. On one occasion, wishing to pass through New Court, Sprocket nipped through the window of the Trust Room, in which Professor Sir James Holt was chairing a meeting. He sauntered past the entire committee, walking over papers along the table. No one turned a hair, and the meeting resumed without undue comment.

When Professor Cameron was appointed Master of Fitzwilliam, he and Mrs Cameron summoned Sprocket to meet their cat in order to avoid future surprise encounters. He was also amongst the college staff who met Professor Cuthbert on his arrival as Master.

The college does collect some repayment for the extravagant hospitality extended to Sprocket, by offering him for the veterinary students' practical revision in their final year. After six or seven medical checkups in a row, he usually retires to Churchill College for a short break in order to restore his journalistic dignity.

Bossuet

Some dons disapproved of his little kitten,
but Peter Bayley was more surprised at the number
of distinguished people who were quite content to
get down on their hands and knees with Bossuet
and a table tennis ball.

Bossuet waits for the postman porter

When Professor Bayley, Fellow of Caius, and a specialist in French, chose the only ginger kitten from a tortoiseshell family, he thought that he was getting a male – female ginger cats being the exception rather than the rule. Only when Bossuet went to the vet for some fine-tuning did he discover his mistake – Bossuet was a lady. By this stage she already had a male name, that of the seventeenth-century Bishop of Condom, Jacques Bénigne-Bossuet, court orator to Louis XIV of France.

Bossuet has an ideal home, living in Peter Bayley's rooms, overlooking both Gonville and Tree Court. Her self-contained and pleasant territory in Tree Court is distinctive in Cambridge for having some trees – a pleasing avenue of whitebeams. Her favourite perch is however in a walnut tree.

A country cat by nature, Bossuet does not venture outside Tree Court, avoiding the mad swirl of people and bicycles flowing constantly past the college gate, and her more crazy feline neighbours. Everything a discriminating cat could require is within the college. As well as the trees, there are shrubs under which she can lurk, a balustrade outside Peter Bayley's rooms that makes a perfect cat maze, and undergraduates to supplement her home care. The gardeners like her, because she doesn't dig up the flower beds, and so do the tourists when she rolls on the path in front of them. The postman porter often stops on his rounds to deliver a tickle or two, and when she sees Peter Bayley coming through the court, she dashes over to him, her tail held high in a curious and jaunty hook shape. Bossuet's only excursions are when she and Peter Bayley travel to his country retreat, where the

The lure of bacon

surrounding fields tempt her to stray rather further than in Cambridge, and where she prefers to have her occasional battles.

Home life is equally luxurious, with open fires to loll by. Bossuet often sits with Peter Bayley in his study, looking critically over his shoulder as he works on his word processor. She occasionally gets at the keyboard herself, but hasn't yet written the definitive miaow. In common with all cats, Bossuet has some odd habits. She won't drink anything other than the stale water from flower vases, which she frequently sends flying. She is manically fond of bacon, and a foolproof way of getting her in is to start frying. She can detect it from anywhere.

Tree Court: Bossuet's favourite haunt

Benson

'Council agreed that **Corrie** (tabby and white,
end of tail missing, sometimes referred to as
"Fat Cat" by students) should be adopted as official
College Cat ... Council established a feline felicity
fund ... to satisfy her alimentary requirements.
Dining rights were given: Class 1(c) (a) (t).'

Outside the Porters' Lodge: Benson takes a break

This was the most momentous Council minute for cats at Jesus College, Cambridge. Corrie belonged to the former Master of Jesus, Sir Alan Cottrell. After Sir Alan retired, taking Corrie with him, she kept returning to Jesus and the students who kept her supplied with chocolate bars and crisps. She became known as the college cat and the case for formal acknowledgment of her status was put by Dr Mika Oldham, also known as the Keeper of the Cat, to a meeting of the College Society and the College Council.

Corrie is still spoken of in legendary terms. A door only had to be opened for her to waddle in, looking eagerly for food or a bed. One night a college visitor half woke during the night, believing that he had suffered a stroke. He became aware, on turning over, of a heaviness in one leg, and had difficulty moving it. On easing himself upright, the sensation disappeared. With some consternation he turned on the light to see the enormous Corrie, flopped on her side, having slid off his leg.

Whilst Sir Alan and Lady Cottrell kept her on a modest diet, Corrie waddled round the college, getting fatter and fatter, until her stomach almost scraped the ground. Viewed from the back she was said to resemble nothing more than an overladen barge, swaying from side to side in an effort to keep upright in a stiff wind. Despite her immense size, she lived for an astonishing twenty-one years and managed to coexist happily with Mephistopheles, the cat of Lord Renfrew, current Master of Jesus.

Corrie is buried in the Fellows' Garden, and will soon have a memorial plaque there. There was a rather bizarre postscript to her demise, reminiscent of the old Ealing Studio comedies. Mika Oldham wanted Corrie buried in the Fellows' Garden, and the vet arranged for her to collect the frozen remains of Corrie in a suitable, but rather distinctive bag. While

walking through college on her way back, she bumped into the Dean, showing round a group of visiting VIP guests. Having been introduced at length to everyone, Mika Oldham was about to make a hasty getaway, when the Dean jokingly asked her what she had in the bag. Muttering something about late shopping, she managed to extricate herself. A Keeper of the Cat has to have a lot of *sang-froid*.

Sam came next, a foundling kitten discovered in Jesus Lane by Mrs Butler, a bedder at the college. She and her family took it on themselves to support Sam, who took up residence in the Lodge and sat, whenever he could, in the upturned top hat that the Head

Benson — feline telephonist

Walking across the 'chimney'

That 'awful cat'

Porter, Peter Bacon, uses for ceremonial occasions at college, resulting in urgent fur removal from time to time.

E. M. Forster wrote, of the approach to Jesus along the 'chimney', a rather plain walled walk, that 'at the end of its calculated dullness rises Alcock's Gate Tower, promising a different world'. The fifteenth-century gate tower, built by the founder, Bishop Alcock, houses the Porters' Lodge, presided over by Peter Bacon. Standing by the counter, it is difficult not to perceive an exceptionally warm and friendly atmosphere. It is like a family drop-in centre, decorated with postcards and family photographs from students

and staff alike. A snoozing tabby cat is usually wrapped around the main telephone, uncaringly inhibiting the activities of Angela Masters, who dashes between operating the telephones and working in the college library.

The cat is Benson. Peter Bacon and Angela Masters told me that he was a new arrival, acquired from the Blue Cross by Dr Oldham in response to requests from the students for a replacement college cat. At present he is in Dr Oldham's care, and has now taken over Corrie's dining rights in college, which entitles him to a food fund. Angela Masters says that Benson is 'not a very nice cat'. He bites. But judging by the cheerful salutations given by undergraduates passing him in the 'chimney', he is rapidly establishing himself as a college feature. I'm sure the young lady who grinned and asked, 'How is the awful cat?', didn't truly mean it. Peter Bacon thinks Benson a funny and quite intelligent cat, and was at pains to point out his initiative in joining a group of conference visitors guided by Mr Griffiths, former Head Porter and informal expert on Thomas Cranmer. Benson sat with earnest attention before meekly following the party through to the Fellows' Garden.

The company of cats at Jesus has been augmented by a feral cat, called Jesus, who lives in the car park. He is apparently almost as fat as Corrie was. Benson and Mephistopheles meet occasionally in the Porters' Lodge, and Benson has to put up with regular visits by Oliver, his ginger neighbour from Wesley House, who has established cordial relations with the gardeners. So far, the two cats have contented themselves with medium-distance growling, but Oliver is not about to relinquish his visitor's rights, nor Benson his newly acquired dining rights.

Looking for Mephistopheles

Olga

A dainty, elegant and extremely aristocratic Russian
Blue named after Olga Korbut, the renowned
Russian gymnast, is the present feline inhabitant of
the Provost's Lodge at King's.

The dainty Olga

Professor Patrick Bateson, Provost of King's, and his wife Dusha moved into the Lodge with quite a retinue of cats – Olga, her daughter Flossie (also a Russian Blue) and four of Olga's kittens. Flossie didn't survive long – she was run over whilst trying to return to her old house in Panton Street. She was found by the President of nearby Queens' College who had two Burmese cats of his own. Believing that he had found one of them – neither was in the house that morning – he took the remains back to Queens' and the family conducted a mournful burial in the gardens. Their cats turned up shortly afterwards, but not in time to console the President, who had already left for Italy. The Batesons ascertained that it was Flossie who had in fact been buried, after which she was left in peace at Queens' College.

Olga's first reaction to the move was to spend six weeks stubbornly dug into the recesses of a bedroom wardrobe, coming out only to drink bathwater and eat a few dry biscuits. Perhaps her emergence from feline depression was due to the expert intervention of Patrick Bateson, an 'ethologist' (zoologist specializing in the study of animal behaviour).

Max and Rosie were acquired to keep Olga company. She loathed them both. They behaved ostentatiously from the start. Rosie sauntered over to Trinity, where one don took such a liking to her that she stayed all weekend. But once more Cambridge traffic struck and Max was run over, leaving Rosie to fall into the clutches of a cat thief.

Dusha Bateson describes the resilient Olga as a pretty promiscuous cat, having produced fifty kittens in ten litters, about half of which were from aristocratic

Lying in wait for Frindle

matings. Her purebred kittens are spread far and wide. One went to New York City, and now resides on East 83rd Street, whilst two of her 'grandkittens' (from Flossie) live across the park in an apartment in the Dakota. Despite being called Lenin and Trotsky, they encountered no undue problems from the US immigration service. The breed make ideal apartment cats, but all three, when taken to their respective summer residences in upstate New York and Maine, abandon dainty midtown manners and respond vigorously to the call of the wild.

Another kitten, Bogomir, went in a large holdall to Italy with a fellow ethologist and family friend, Bruno D'Udine. Olga's last kitten went to Amsterdam – a city whose liberal reputation might well have attracted Olga!

For many people, King's College is the epitome of Cambridge. Its grand scale was conceived by the founder, Henry VI, and the view from the Backs, of the chapel and eighteenth-century Gibbs Building is instantly recognizable. The foundation of the college was linked to Eton, provider of the King's Scholars, and the two institutions have been closely linked since, with the King's choristers still wearing traditional Eton collars and top hats. Only in the latter part of the nineteenth-century were non-Etonian scholars admitted.

The one-time tradition whereby degrees were awarded to students without the tedium of an exam may still provoke nostalgia in some undergraduates. For the time being, however, their studies are only interrupted by Olga, shrieking furiously as she beats the living daylights out of Frindle, a neighbouring cat. I watched as college office windows closed discreetly.

Olga and a famous view

Thomasina, Socks and Puss

Some while ago I came across a book called
The Philosopher Cat, and had been curious to
meet Thomasina, the cat that had inspired
such a loving endeavour.

Thomasina plans her day's social calls

My curiosity was even more aroused when I heard that the Pembroke cat, also known as 'The Office Cat', shared the college site with a litter mate called Socks, 'The Garden Cat'. I then found out that there was *another* cat belonging to the Master and his wife. According to Dr James Hickson, Fellow of Pembroke and Director of Medical and Veterinary Studies, Thomasina believes that the college, founded in 1347 by Marie de Valence, widow of the Earl of Pembroke, exists entirely for her benefit.

She arrived as a kitten, in the wake of her sister Socks, who had been brought to the college by the Head Gardener, Nicholas Firman. The Tutor's secretary and the admissions secretary of the time had asked to have a cat and, when they knew that the new kitten was from the same litter as Socks, hoped for a tom to make a properly balanced pair. James Hickson made arrangements for both cats to go to the School of Veterinary Clinical Medicine for appropriate adjustments, at which point it became clear that both adjustments were going to have to be gynaecological.

The new office kitten had been treated like a male, and had begun to play in a distinctly unladylike way. James Hickson's name for 'him' was Growltiger, but others suggested Thomas Gray, the eighteenth-century poet who lived at Pembroke for most of his life. This was the name that stuck. When the mistake in gender was uncovered, Thomas became Thomasina.

The little cat was beset by visiting hedgehogs. They left spoor for which she was blamed, and snuffled their way through Thomasina's saucer of bread and milk, while she danced around them, in banshee-like rage.

These days the saucers of milk left outside certain doors provide a map of her regular stops because, apart from lolling around the college offices, Thomasina does a lot of visiting. At about six o' clock each evening, she joins the undergraduates for their buffet supper, usually poking a whisker round the kitchen door. The window behind High Table is another regular calling point, possibly due to the attentions of a generous waiter. She also joins them for some pretty boisterous undergraduate gatherings.

Her vast array of feeding opportunities causes her to swell dramatically in term-time. Even when food supplies dwindle, she consoles herself with a plentiful supply of cat biscuits, sent to her by Sir Thomas Adams, Professor of Arabic, and his wife.

Thomasina is also an honorary member of the college Science Society, where she has a proxy vote. The Library Cats' Society of Minnesota invited her to become a member, and Thomasina duly calls regularly at the college library, from where she is sent packing lest she be locked up for the night.

In the summer Thomasina spends more time in the gardens of Second Court, where she sometimes crouches near two large mallards, wriggling her hips in a show of aggression. That is as far as her duck hunting gets, as the mallards are roughly twice her size. Occasionally, Thomasina and Socks meet in the garden, and sit, face to face across an invisible dividing line, growling unconvincingly before turning their backs on one another. James Hickson, intrigued one day by the apparent spontaneous agitation of branches

The Library cat

in the Judas tree, found Thomasina up one branch, a visiting cat up another, conducting a vigorous exchange of views.

Generally the Pembroke gardens and grounds provide a peaceful haunt for the office and garden cats. This feline accord may be in part due to the influence of the third Pembroke cat.

Puss, the cat of the Master's wife, Lady Margaret Tomkys, lives in the Master's Lodge. Puss accompanied the family on a number of Sir Roger Tomkys'

A gentle retirement for Puss

diplomatic tours. First she went by car to Rome, causing only one moment of panic when, at a rest stop beside a French autoroute she slipped her specially made harness. Her apartment in Rome afforded some interesting opportunities to adopt a different way of life, and she became a high-level cat, teetering around the tiled roofs of the Palazzo Ricci, thereby avoiding the rapacious attentions of various mean and feisty Roman street cats.

In Bahrain, Puss took to a cupboard for six weeks before entering into delicate negotiations with more wild cats who left their kittens in the safety of the gardens. Air conditioning provided the necessary relief from the humidity of summer.

From Bahrain, the family flew, with Puss, to Jordan and thence by road to Syria, where Puss calmly took up her normal routine in Damascus. The breakdown of diplomatic relations between Britain and Syria saw Puss hastily evacuated to London and six months' quarantine.

Shortly after, the family was on the move again, this time to the High Commission in Kenya. Puss went too, on the assumption that she would probably end her days in Nairobi. However, outliving all expectations, she returned with the family to England, surviving a second period of quarantine, and lives in gentle and well-deserved retirement at Pembroke.

Daisy

Previously dragooned into posing for a calendar, Daisy was reluctant to sit for me. So her owner, Lady Ann English, gave her Hobson's choice — no choice at all — by shutting her in a room with me.

Daisy surrenders to the camera

Hobson's choice

This famous English expression arose in connection with St Catherine's College. Thomas Hobson operated from there as University carrier in the sixteenth- and early seventeenth-century, providing horses for the journey to and from London. As travellers invariably wanted the fastest animal, he gave them the most rested horse in the stable – choice didn't enter into it.

Daisy is a relatively new arrival at St Catherine's – known locally as Cat's – but lived about a mile away from the college for several years. Her home with Sir Terence, Master of St Catherine's and eminent heart surgeon, and his wife Ann, is in the Master's Lodge, overlooking Queens' College. The Lodge is a Victorian building, at the back of the main college buildings that were seventeenth-century replacements, for the earlier medieval buildings of St Catherine's Hall, founded by the third Provost of King's College in 1473.

Daisy succeeded Coala, who came from a garden fete for the NSPCC, held at the Englishes' former home. Their daughter Katharine, showing some initiative on being refused permission to get a kitten, persuaded a friend to lend her fifty pence so that she could buy a small black specimen, who moved into the territory of Alpha, the family dog, curling up every night to sleep with him. Coala completely flouted the kitten ban by producing more than sixty herself.

Daisy waits for Beta

Her patience wears thin

Towards the end of Coala's life, the two daughters acquired another kitten for their father. It is unusual to find a female ginger cat, and extremely unusual for them to breed, but Daisy, in keeping with Coala's example, did just that. It was only when the vet saw her that he told Lady English that Daisy was in fact a 'British Red'.

The whereabouts of her first litter was a complete mystery. Every night she would appear for food, but there was no sign of the kittens. Daisy obligingly accompanied the family in their attempts to locate them, poking her nose into empty cupboards and the like. One day she was spied, creeping through some shrubs surrounding an old dead elm tree. Perhaps mindful of Sir Terence's strictures, she had prudently borne and kept her litter in the hollowed tree top. Another litter was produced more conventionally, on the doormat.

Daisy also has a dog friend Beta, an affable and enthusiastic King Charles Spaniel puppy, with whom she arrived at St Catherine's. She had given her a very frosty reception as a puppy, enticing Beta to her, then giving her a clout around the ears. Beta still follows her happily into the garden, watching every movement she makes with unrequited admiration. When Daisy was first allowed out of the Master's Lodge, after three weeks of confinement, she promptly disappeared. Ann English told me that every day she expected a phone call from the City Cleansing Department – the phone call all cat owners dread – instead of which Daisy turned up after ten days, early in the morning with the milk. Where she went was a mystery, but it rather lessened Beta's hero worship. Now Daisy has to be fed on a shelf to prevent Beta from snaffling her food, and gets chased up trees by the dog, in line with convention. Daisy seems to enjoy this, however, hanging from a branch, taunting Beta.

Having faced many a reluctant cat, I have evolved a fairly effective technique for dealing with them – cold indifference. After about an hour without attention Daisy posed for a short while. She briefly came into the garden too, but our concentration was disturbed by the enthusiastic attention of Beta.

Caiaphas

A porter in a neighbouring college,
when asked about Caiaphas, muttered,
'Don't talk to me about *that* cat.'

One of several female cats in this book with a male name, Caiaphas also shares the distinction of having been regularly nominated – unsuccessfully – for Junior Common Room elections. She probably failed because she has too many outside commitments.

This incorrigibly peripatetic cat sometimes irritates her owner, George Bush, Chaplain of St John's, who would frankly like to see more of her. He maintains that she was a perfectly normal kitten, and attributes her wanderlust to the car crash she caused by leaping out of her box onto his lap on her first journey.

Before coming to Cambridge she lived in harmony with her kittens, Herod and Pontius, for two years, which seems to have exhausted her goodwill towards other cats.

Taking its name from the medieval hospital of St John the Evangelist, on the site of which it was built, St John's competes with Trinity as one of the largest of the Cambridge colleges, and certainly occupies the largest Oxbridge site. The gatehouse in St John's Street, with its colourful brickwork surrounding the heraldic arms of the college founder, Lady Margaret Beaufort, is one of the most attractive in Cambridge.

A better home for a cat is hard to imagine, but to

Caiaphas: an unusually still moment

describe St John's as the *home* of Caiaphas is misleading. It is more like an expeditionary base camp. Like a feline 'conquistador', she regularly vaults over to adjoining Trinity, and also journeys further afield. George Bush has had to make several journeys to retrieve his colonizing cat. Once she was at King's: very disloyal, given the musical rivalry between the colleges' choirs. Following an earlier disruption of a service in St John's, by running around the chapel making the choristers giggle, she took an abrupt fortnight's sabbatical at Churchill.

She does like to be included in events, and has lined up with the celebrants during undergraduate services. In the course of one of George Bush's particularly penetrating sermons, she hurled herself into his arms.

The most enjoyable rescue trip was to Caius, where she had spent a long weekend with a College Fellow. A fine Sauternes was the consolation offered George Bush when he went to fetch her. He rather regrets that Caiaphas hasn't made Caius a regular port of call. Apparently she has gone off King's since hearing a former Archbishop of Canterbury preach in the college chapel.

In St John's itself, a large rota of undergraduates are familiar with Caiaphas's 'open the door' howl, as she knows all the comfortable beds. George Bush, however, remembers a hideously embarrassing experience at High Table one night. The butler courteously enquired as to his choice of evening repast. He chose the cold beef. The butler coughed, bent discreetly down, and informed him with no little disapproval that Caiaphas had eaten it all earlier.

A misleading air of innocence

En route for tea at Trinity

Burbage, Armin and Muffet –
Darius and Jedburgh

Isaac Newton, one of the most famous of
Trinity Fellows, had two cat flaps installed,
for his 'greater' and 'lesser' cats.

Miss Muffet and Burbage: a life of academic luxury

Jedburgh leads Darius on a short stroll

How appropriate that this, the largest of the University colleges, also has the largest and most varied concentration of cats. Anne Barton, Professor of English and Fellow of the college has three Somalis – Burbage, after the great Shakespearean actor, Armin, after a Shakespearean clown, and Thaisa (aka Muffet), after the queen in Shakespeare's *Pericles*. Her fourth Somali, Tarlton (named after an Elizabethan clown) was run over at her country home. He had led a sociable village life, attending the local primary school, an old people's home, and the village pub, on the way to which he was struck down. Anne Barton was left with a melancholy Miss Muffet.

Burbage was introduced as consoling company. Miss Muffet took an instant and vehement dislike to him. Armin came, in an effort to enliven both cats. Muffet took an instant and vehement dislike to him. The only advantage was that she became slightly more kindly disposed towards Burbage.

This turbulent trio eventually arrived at Trinity, and reside in pleasant airy Jacobean rooms, over cloisters that form part of the early seventeenth-century court built by Thomas Nevile, then master of Trinity. They are not outdoor cats, although they indulge in some heart-stopping parapet walking, eyeing with keen interest the roof of Wren's great library building. But when one is the recipient of three splendid meals a day, the tendency is to stick around in case one of the others gets there first.

As soon as Anne arrived at Trinity she was made aware of the resident cat population. A burly, hard-hunting Burmese, by the name of Stevenson, breezed

Clown and Actor: Armin and Burbage

Muffet: *Least turbulent of the Trinity trio*

A moment of stage fright for Burbage

in as she was unpacking, enraged that his owner Tony Weir, Law Fellow at Trinity, had had the temerity to go away without him. Even when his owner returned, Stevenson stayed on a few extra days just to make a point.

Just along the court from Anne Barton lives Dr Hazel McLean, Trinity Fellow, and Director of Law Studies. Hazel McLean's husband, Bernard, had been utterly captivated by Stevenson, and in response she

purchased two Blue Burmese kittens, Darius and Jedburgh. Her husband's infatuation with Stevenson waned slightly when he learnt of Stevenson's early morning attack on the two terrified cats, which came to a dramatic climax with Darius and Jedburgh cowering in the bathtub, whilst Hazel McLean, abandoning the restraint vital to a lawyer, forced Stevenson back onto the staircase with a broom handle. On learning of his cat's iniquitous incursion, Tony Weir graciously donated a hydraulic water pistol as a deterrent against future aggression. Stevenson did eventually accept the newcomers, and lived out his days at Trinity in regal splendour.

In the meantime, as a consequence of an accident at the vet's, Jedburgh lost her sight. Hazel McLean and her husband were in despair. Jedburgh had been the runt of the litter, born with a broken tail, and had nearly died at three months as the result of a viral infection. Precautions were taken to make life easier for her, none of which turned out to be necessary. Jedburgh is a real fighter, and with some assistance from Darius she has re-negotiated her way around college. She still hops onto the laps of unsuspecting students, and has an uncanny knack of landing on their essays just as Hazel McLean is writing her final comments. The supplementary pawprint is regarded as quite a prize. Watching Jedburgh outside is uncanny. She functions in a way indistinguishable from that of a sighted cat, manoeuvring through stone balustrades, and stalking confidently along the cloisters.

Darius is gentler and calmer than Jedburgh, although she shows a venturesome spirit once outside. She sometimes gets stranded on top of the Master's garden wall, doubly hazardous, as she runs the risk of attracting the attention of another Trinity cat – Titan. Few student beds have not been graced by this huge tabby. Titan eats anything, and loves everyone – apart from Darius when she strays into his territory. I never caught sight of Titan, but knew he was around, as he'd left a rather unappealing collection of ingredients for pigeon pie in Great Court, by the fountain that once supplied the college drinking water.

There are neighbourly associations. Titan goes down the Backs. Olga, from nearby King's College has popped in for a weekend break, and readers, knowing how close St John's is, will have no trouble in guessing the identity of another regular visitor.

Cats with literary leanings

Lloyd, Peggotty and Oliver

I had never before admitted the possibility
of a feline ghost, but the three cats of
Wesley House have no doubt that
Two Stroke's ghost is still around.

Two Stroke belonged to a former student of Wesley House, the Methodist theological college founded in 1921. This hard-purring, hard-hitting tom was the bane of the other Wesley cats' lives. Before Lloyd the college porter's cat knew better, he would walk in the court only to be set upon by Two Stroke. His brother, Henry (named after the British boxer Henry Cooper), acted as bodyguard. In a flurry of flying fur, with Lloyd looking on from behind a pillar, Henry and Two Stroke would eventually separate, sometimes taking days to recover.

On good days in the summer when there are tourists around, Lloyd will sometimes venture out. He enjoys the attention of American visitors particularly. Oliver and Peggotty, the Principal's Lodge cats, are even more circumspect. They have a quick look around, staying within instant flight range of their front door. Unlike Lloyd they have the advantage of a back garden. All three cats twitch nervously when they leave their homes, and the slightest breath of wind stirring the shrubs is enough to send them fleeing in terror.

Oliver and Peggotty are the third set of ginger cats to belong to the College Principal, Dr Ivor Jones and his family. One of their predecessors, Mitton, had the misfortune to run up against Toast, the infamous Lincoln Cathedral Cat, and although he didn't make it to Wesley House his successor Smintheus did, establishing the precedent of being a Jesus College visitor – a mantle that was eventually handed on to Oliver.

Oliver and Peggotty, two ginger litter mates, were acquired through the services of the Cats' Protection League. According to Dr Jones, they were particularly captivating, so much so that in response to an

Peggotty and Oliver: watching for the ghost of Two Stroke

An apprehensive Lloyd makes sure the coast is clear

advertisement from a local photographer, they were entered into a beautiful kitten competition. Both were taken along to the studio, where the photographer had carefully prepared his lights and erected suitable backgrounds. It took them less than half an hour to wreck the studio. The backgrounds were shredded, lights were askew, and the photographer, with his two shop assistants, was trying to prevent the two kittens from dashing through rolls of carpet. They were finally dragged out and returned to Wesley in disgrace. They didn't win the contest.

The cats gradually mellowed. Peggotty became a homebody and got so fed up with the large number of visitors coming to the Principal's Lodge that she had to be treated for stress. Oliver sabotaged meetings by crunching dead birds outside the window. He befriended the Jesus College gardeners, whom he often joins for lunch. His visits extend to the far side of the grounds, an extensive territory for a cat, but he has been trained to come in response to a whistle. As Dr Jones returns from visiting the organ scholars at Jesus, Oliver sometimes leaps out of the bushes to join him on his homeward walk.

Oliver en route to lunch at Jesus College

Jessica and Charlie

Jessica is likely to be the only college cat actually to read this book. The reason for this lies in her secret life, which came as a considerable surprise to her owner.

Jessica: fetched under protest from a nearby bookshop

Jessica and her brother Charlie live with Philipa King, her young brother Jason and a dog called Hattie Darling, in a small apartment adjacent to the main quadrangle. A few days after their arrival, Jessica took to leaving the rooms early, not reappearing until the early evening. The cat returned in good spirits, and the outings became a matter of routine. After a year Philipa's curiosity could no longer be restrained, and having seen Jessica slink over the back wall of Westcott, she dashed down a narrow lane in time to catch a glimpse of the cat streaking up a staircase at the back of a row of shops.

An obliging Charlie makes sure he's not going too fast

her attention towards a well-appointed cat basket wedged firmly against a radiator, in which Jessica, yawning widely, was firmly ensconced. An astounded Philipa was told that the cat had been a regular visitor over the last year, and was normally admitted by Martin Fabb, the Graphics Buyer, whose arrival the ingenious Jessica would await each morning. Paul Bishop-Culpepper, the Deputy Manager, has even installed a key – with a fob in the form of a cat – on the main keyboard, so that the staff are aware as to whether she is 'in' or 'out'.

Charlie, on the other hand, stays at home and likes to attend chapel with Philipa at Westcott House, an 'approved society' rather than a college within the University. It was founded for the purpose of training clergy in 1881 by the then Regius Professor of Divinity at Cambridge, Brooke Foss Westcott. Despite his religious leanings Philipa thinks Charlie is not very bright, I thought him slightly saucy. He insinuated himself into an outdoor service, sat demurely in the preacher's chair during the homily, and pricked up his ears at salient points, thoroughly sabotaging the solemnity of the occasion. His owner was singing in the choir, and was thus in no position to remove Charlie even if she had wanted to.

He likes to go for walks with Philipa and Hattie the dog, and can often be seen strolling alongside as they walk through the town. I took his part firstly, because his laid-back nature made him marvellously easy to photograph and secondly, because his sister, far from being literary is immensely idle.

Following her, Philipa found herself in the arts and graphics branch of a well-known Cambridge book-shop. Had anybody, she tentatively enquired, seen a cat come in? Several of the staff looked up and directed

Charlie looks for Philipa and Hattie the dog

Sammy and Rosie

If Dr Johnson thought it 'a great thing to dine with the Canons of Christ Church', how could I resist the opportunity to pass time with a Canon's cats?

Sammy, caught at last

Rosie prefers Marian Ward's study

I first visited Keith and Marian Ward whilst researching *Cathedral Cats*. Our meeting took place in one of a
row of seventeenth-century Canon's houses on the
North side of the main quadrangle – 'Tom Quad' –
overlooking the Mercury fountain. The buildings were
inspired by Cardinal Wolsey (initial founder of the
college as Cardinal College in 1525), and his architect, Henry Redman. After Wolsey's fall from grace,
Henry VIII refounded 'The House' as King Henry
VIII's College.

I remembered my first visit to meet Sammy and
Rosie, and how frustrating it had been to have to
admit defeat in such a magnificent setting. Both cats
had taken one look at me and fled in different direc-
tions. Fate decreed that their escape was only temporary, however, because *College Cats* clearly gave me a
chance for a return match.

The Wards greeted me so warmly that I was imme-
diately suspicious. The cats were nowhere to be seen.
Sammy was actually wedged behind my chair, whilst
Rosie slept in Marian's study. The cats' nervousness
was not without foundation. When they had first
come to Christ Church, builders were at work. Rosie's
first act was to leap in terror onto the top of a kitchen
unit housing a built-in oven only to find, as she
plummeted to the floor behind that there *was* no top.
A hole was cut through an adjacent kitchen unit, from
which a bedraggled, dusty and protesting cat was
eventually extracted.

With the welcome departure of the builders,

Sammy and Rosie tentatively started to explore their new home. The Wards had turned one of the upstairs rooms into a studio for their artist son, who habitually left his palette on the floor, a practice that only came to light after Sammy, inspired perhaps by Jackson Pollock, left several trails of footprints in Burnt and Raw Sienna up and down the stairs.

Rosie attempted a rather more spectacular staircase stunt. This entailed stretching through the banisters at the top of a stairwell, to the banisters at the other side of the landing. An eight-inch kitten cannot bridge a three-foot gap, and Rosie took her second plunge, this time descending some forty feet. There was a huge thump at the bottom, and a moment of horrified silence before Rosie unsteadily picked herself up, shaken but otherwise unhurt.

The cats' reluctance to go outside has now been tackled. Marian Ward decided to take them into the garden at the back of the house. At first both Sammy and Rosie hung on to Marian like grim death, only releasing her when they all went in again, but gradually both cats found that, in the absence of builders, the outside world has some merit. Rosie meanders around, occasionally meeting Maisy, the Cathedral Cat belonging to the Dean, whilst Sammy has found the underground sixteenth-century Canon's brewhouse to be an ideal place for meeting the bossy Siamese belonging to a neighbouring Russian don.

Curiosity overcame Sammy's nerves

Simpkins

'Now Simpkins is purr-fect!', ran the caption in the *Oxford Star*, under a large photograph of the Hertford College cat, being held by one of the students.

Simpkins demands attention

Weed's old territory

This self-assured cat lives in a college that stands at the very centre of the medieval university. Hart Hall, founded by Elias de Hertford, is first mentioned at the end of the thirteenth-century, and provided accommodation for students. It had mixed fortunes, being dissolved at the beginning of the eighteenth-century, due to lack of money, and was taken over by Magdalen Hall, who built the new Georgian front on Catte Street. Towards the latter part of the century a new benefaction by Thomas Baring made it possible for Magdalen Hall to be recreated as Hertford College.

Simpkins is not the first cat at Hertford. Sir Geoffrey Warnock, a past College Principal, had two. One, Sir G, was by all accounts a beautiful white cat with a tabby tail, so beautiful that the night porter once spotted and gave chase to a man who had scooped up Sir G in the street and dropped him into a sack. Sadly he disappeared for ever shortly afterwards. Sir Geoffrey also gave a home to a stray, found under a van parked outside the college. The poor thing was so spindly, that the only suitable name was 'Weed'.

Despite his lack of stature, there was no question that he should have a successor when he passed on. A former student offered Simpkins, a small black and white kitten. He quickly assumed total dominance of the college, colonizing the Front and New Quadrangle. When I visited he was circling the quad, pretending to sit in the sun outside the college offices while sizing up the chance of a lethal leap onto some unsuspecting bird in the nearby shrubs. On one occasion he tried to take on a pair of mallards, regular college visitors. Soon after he was seen in full retreat, pursued by a large and very angry drake.

Simpkins had needed a small operation to ensure that no more tiny Simpkins would be running around the college grounds. The students, with whom Simpkins is pretty popular, decided to raise the money for the operation amongst themselves, by donating ten pence every time somebody swore. The fourteen pounds was raised in record time.

Avoiding the drakes

Simpkins was good friends with Rosie, a cat of similar appearance belonging to the Bursar of New College. Unfortunately they always got their visiting times mixed up. Rosie would zip through to the Lodge to see if Simpkins was in, just as Simpkins was busy making his way to New College. One day he disappeared without trace. It transpired that the college darts team had taken him as mascot to a match at St Edmund Hall. Simpkins got himself locked in the library while the team were carousing after the match. They forgot to retrieve him.

On patrol in Front Quad

Now when he feels ignored Simpkins haunts the Lodge, sitting on the counter, staring disapprovingly at the source of his neglect. If that doesn't work, he'll move down to the desk, planting himself firmly on top of any urgently required paperwork. Failing that, he'll sprawl out where he is most likely to trip someone up.

The darts team's mascot

Outside the library

Echo and Europa

As kittens, Echo and Europa would scale their owner's trouser legs using their needle-like claws. His cries would startle visitors into believing that a moment of Archimedean insight had taken place.

Echo and Europa still enjoy a good tutorial

Echo contemplates the disappearing garden

In short, Echo and Europa created mayhem. Some of the undergraduates took full advantage of their mischevious nature during particularly demanding tutorials – a surreptitiously jiggled pencil would entice both cats to leap into the middle of the table, scattering papers in every direction.

Dr Ian Archer is Tutor in History at Keble College Oxford. He had to ask twice before he was allowed to give a home to the kittens, although the Bursar stoutly maintains that he only mentioned a cat, not cats. They came to the college eighteen months ago from a distinguished academic and cat-intensive household. There had been some reports by students of mice around the college, and Echo and Europa have caught a fair few in the Fellows' Garden, directly outside Ian

Archer's apartment. To their dismay, the college embarked on a major construction programme of student accommodation, taking a large chunk of the garden with it.

Now Echo and Europa wander in the direction of the modern quad, where the main attraction seems to be the beer barrels outside the Junior Common Room. Perhaps they are affected by the alcoholic fumes, because their feeding habits have become very unpredictable. They know what they like, rather like A. A. Milne's Tigger, but ... it changes. One day it is tinned rabbit and Ian dutifully goes off to buy a large consignment. At the next meal it is chicken rather than rabbit. Along comes another box. They suddenly realize that they meant beef. As a consequence, Ian

Archer's store cupboard resembles a catfood warehouse more than a don's pantry.

Recently Europa has been stalking off in high dudgeon to visit the Senior Dean and Ian Archer wonders whether she is trying to tell him that if he doesn't keep the standards up, there are others who will appreciate her better. On the other hand, when the cats have been banished for being over-boisterous, they scramble up onto the flat roof, and track Ian Archer as he moves from room to room through the many skylights. Nothing, he says, is more disconcerting when relaxing in the bath than to see the shadowy outlines of two cats staring morosely down at him though the skylight.

Europa considers defecting

Suki

I had come to see Suki, who was dozing on a settee
in the living room. She very obligingly clambered
over onto my lap. Then I caught a glimpse of a
white cat streaking by my feet. That, said Anne
Longshawe, Housekeeper at Linacre College, was
Snowy. I asked how the two of them got on, and
she told me that Suki, although well domesticated,
barely tolerated the other cats. Cats? I thought.

The bathroom cat: a short-lived break for Tabitha

Suki gives an ultimatum

Then another white cat sneaked past me from the opposite direction to Snowy. This was Smarty, named for her extraordinary yellow and blue eyes. There is a dog, Sherry, too but she had been taken out for a walk by Mr Longshawe. I asked Mrs Longshawe if she was absolutely sure there were no more cats. Only the bathroom cat, she said.

What would be next? A boot cupboard cat? Maybe a pantry cat, a curtain cat, or perhaps a 'spare' cat? But no, that was it. I resolved to find out more later.

When Suki came, she was almost wild, and there is still something of the feral cat in the shape of her head. Snowy and Smarty are sisters, and most visitors only see the briefest flashes of white, zipping from one room to another, scrupulously avoiding Suki.

There is a pleasant garden at Linacre, which borders on the University Parks, and the two white cats often startle themselves into leaping over the garden wall. Suki also haunted the Parks in her younger years but now prefers lying in the middle of the car park.

The bathroom cat was called Tabitha and came from Mrs Longshawe's daughter. The company of three dogs had made her unhappy. Sadly the two cats – Snowy and Smarty – proved to be just as unwelcoming. Consequently, Tabitha chose to live happily in the bathroom, where her food is served twice daily. She has a comfortable chair, and never leaves the bathroom except to go out, at which time she risks all in a high-speed dash for the cat flap at the other end of the corridor. Tabitha stays in the garden, but has recently shown a penchant for scaffolding – probably because it keeps her out of reach of her confrères.

Mrs Longshawe's son is the college Head Chef. I could picture the cats licking their lips in anticipation of the latest offerings to come from the kitchen. Not a bit of it. He doesn't like cats.

Smarty, named for her multicoloured eyes

Another tense garden encounter

Polly Flinders

Some cats just don't know their own luck. Oriel
College's plans for emergency evacuation include a
scheme for the safe removal of college cat Polly
Flinders. Dr Catto, her original mentor, devoted
considerable time and thought to it.

Polly Flinders: *a last minute reprieve*

Coming up from the old cellar

Polly Flinders came to the Nicholson family as a thirteenth birthday present for daughter Jane. Life was good for her at the family home in North Oxford. Then came a major crisis.

The Revd Dr Ernest Nicholson, due to take up the position of Provost of Oriel, didn't know whether the college would welcome a cat. Despite support and reassurance from Dr Catto, historian and Fellow of Oriel, it was reluctantly decided that she should be found another home. This so depressed the family that Dr Nicholson decided at the eleventh hour that Polly Flinders should have a probationary period.

In fact she loved her new home tucked away in a corner of Front Quad, and after a short appraisal, began to venture further. Nowadays, if she can't get back into the Provost's Lodge after a night stroll round Oriel Square, the Porters' Lodge makes a convenient alternative. The Head Porter, she discovered, was a soft touch, always ready to give up his chair.

Oriel was founded by Edward II in 1326, and was the University's first royal foundation. There is almost nothing left of the medieval buildings, the college having been rebuilt in the early part of the seventeenth-century. Fortunately, the style of rebuilding retained the medieval spirit, and is a striking example of Gothic workmanship.

Underneath the Provost's Lodgings there are old cellars, in which remnants of the foundations of the original College Hall are to be found. It is here that Polly Flinders made a nocturnal nest, lying curled up as close to the heating boiler as she could get without actually bursting into flames. A magnetic cat flap was installed in the disused coal shute, so that she could come and go as she pleased. This arrangement worked well until one of Polly Flinders' male friends opened the flap with brute force, leaving pungent reminders of his affections throughout the Lodge. The cat flap was speedily disabled.

Polly Flinders is not particularly concerned who she interrupts. Having learnt which windows looked in on frequently used rooms, she once tried desperately to attract the attention of Dr Nicholson, who was sitting in his study with ex-President Cossiga of Italy – an Honorary Fellow of Oriel. They were discussing the inauguration of the Fiat-Serena Chair of Italian Studies. No amount of pacing back and forth, pleading stares or silent miaowing could elicit any response, and it was at that point Polly discovered the effectiveness of raking her claws over glass. The meeting was suspended amid much amusement to admit an indignant Polly Flinders.

Underneath the study windows

Oscar

When Oscar went missing during Rag Week, marauding undergraduate catnappers were under suspicion. A thorough search of the college and surroundings by the 'Oscar team' was abandoned, and Radio Oxford was asked to broadcast an SOS appeal.

Oscar keeps in with the Head Gardener

On the lookout for the President's dog

At the eleventh hour, a junior member of the college was enjoying a pre-Christmas drink with friends in a nearby pub, when Oscar strolled in. Delighted to see a familiar face, and purring loudly, he allowed himself to be carried back to the safety of college. Not usually a wandering cat, he sometimes disappears for a night, returning in an exhausted state the next day after some passionate rooftop encounter.

The tradition of cats at St John's stems from Sir Richard Southern, whose foundling cat, Grace, a familiar sight around the college, supplied a number of college staff with kittens. On retiring from the college, Sir Richard and Lady Southern took Grace with them to live in a nearby house. They became concerned that Grace would try to get back to college by herself, risking life and limb crossing St Giles, and suggested that she should return to St John's as the college cat.

Grace's death at a great age upset the whole college and the Domestic Bursar in desperation looked for another cat. After a long and almost fruitless search, a local vet found Oscar, a ginger tom.

Oscar, like his predecessor, was a country cat, and took to the college gardens with glee. He worked out the whereabouts of the most comfortable plants for catnapping, mostly tough heathers. This proved a prudent choice as Oscar relies on the Head Gardener to provide Christmas turkey.

The domestic team who had shown such solicitous regard for Grace now dedicated their energies to Oscar, whose feeding station is at the base of one of the staircases. The same student who had been devoted to Grace was only too pleased to be able to offer Oscar a similar standard of accommodation, and before long the cat became a familiar sight around the contemporary Sir Thomas White Quadrangle.

Around the same time, Oscar had a little problem with the President of the Middle Common Room. Oscar and he did not see eye to eye about anything. A particular bone of contention was the occasional dead bird found on the student's doorstep, about which Oscar made a convincing display of innocence. An attempt was made to ban Oscar from the MCR. The Oscar team, by this time alerted by a potential threat to their charge, rallied round. Urgent lobbying, and some clandestine gatherings around the quad resulted in the hasty election of Oscar to lifetime membership of the MCR.

The only other potential hazard for Oscar now is the College President's dog. He accordingly restricts himself to the newer parts of the college, avoiding the Canterbury Quadrangle, an interesting blend of original fifteenth- and seventeenth-century architecture. This is a little frustrating as he is addicted to posing for tourists' photographs, and can't do it in the oldest and most picturesque part of the college.

A lifetime member of the MCR

Charlie

On the few occasions when Charlie has slipped from Bulwarks Lane into St Peter's College, the Bursar, porters and occasionally students have given hot pursuit. Charlie, cornered and exhausted, gives up the race and is reluctantly returned to her home.

Charlie arrived by subterfuge

Treading carefully in the garden

She has not yet worked out a way to scale the high stone walls that separate the college from her home in the Master's Lodgings, the impressive nineteenth-century former headquarters of the Oxford Canal Company.

The Master, Dr Barron, is an accomplished gardener, and when the family lived in London made it quite clear to his family that cats and good gardens simply did not go together. Daughter Helen desperately wanted a cat, so went off to select a kitten, which was then conveniently given to her by a friend as a 'surprise' birthday present.

Many of Dr Barron's premonitions came true. Charlie blandly ignored the strict guidelines as to where she was permitted to go. So at ease was she that she regularly nipped in through the bedroom window at night to introduce her boyfriend, a large jovial ginger cat. Sadly it was an unrequited feline passion, as Charlie had been neutered. She and her ginger beau were reluctantly parted in preparation for the move to Oxford.

St Peter's College is one of the youngest of the University colleges, founded in 1928 as a permanent private hall by Francis Chavasse, Bishop of Liverpool,

attaining full collegiate status in 1961. Upon Dr
Barron's appointment as Master, he decided to put his
foot down with Charlie, restricting her to the corri-
dors of the Master's Lodgings. Once again, Charlie
flouted the rules. She plays and hunts in the beautiful
terraced garden, and makes night expeditions to the
castle mound.

She enjoys social occasions, but one Christmas
proved too much for her. The family and friends were
gathered in the drawing room for some impromptu
musical entertainment. A counter-tenor struck up a
song with great gusto. Charlie was strolling past the
open door, and leapt in the air as if struck by light-
ning, and then froze. She peered anxiously in, with-
drawing hastily after a minute or two. Struggling to
reach a decision as to what should be done, she then
made a mad dash through the door towards the
singer. His performance faltered momentarily as he
saw the cat patting his leg and whimpering. Charlie
then bounded out of the room, but was unable to stay
away and repeated the whole sequence three or four
times until the song finished. She had never heard a
counter-tenor before.

Otherwise Christmas is an abundant time for
Charlie, as a deluge of specially prepared cat choco-
lates, kitty Christmas puddings and other delights
arrive from the United States, courtesy of the god-
mother of Helen's sister, Catherine.

In spite of his initial reservations, one hopes that Dr
Barron feels a certain benevolence towards Charlie.
She and I walked in the garden one afternoon, and the
beautifully tended terraces of spring flowers suggested
that cats and gardens can coexist after all.

Definitely a tone-deaf cat

Diplock

Diplock's name – that of a notorious executing judge – was acquired as a result of his contribution to pest control at Worcester. This has also made him the recipient of a small maintenance fund, officially allocated by the college's domus committee.

Diplock: the ever moving cat

No one knows exacty how Diplock came to Worcester. Some say he escaped from a barge on the canal that borders the western boundaries of the college gardens. Others believe that he was related to cats belonging to an Emeritus Fellow. Looked after at first by the kitchen staff, he eased his way into college life, and was befriended by Heidi Carlton, College Housekeeper, who feeds him morning and evening with devoted regularity. At first I thought there were four cats at Worcester. A college scout, who also looks after him when Heidi is unavailable, has named him Bruno, whilst the Emeritus Fellow, from whose Burmese cat Diplock is rumoured to have descended, knew him as Maldaevia. Heidi called him Baby.

Diplock has no apparent identity crisis, and follows a pretty cosseted college routine. However, notwithstanding his nomination as a candidate for President, his welcome in the Middle Common Room does vary. He can frequently be found stubbornly snoozing in the most comfortable armchair. There are times when the door is opened and a sleepy but indignant Diplock is firmly ejected. He prowls the warren of staircases in the Terraces, selecting his room for the night, and then howls plaintively outside until admitted. Diplock also exploits the hospitality of the various college houses adjoining the main site.

Master of twenty-six acres

Worcester College was founded in 1741, as the result of a benefaction from Sir Thomas Cookes, a Worcestershire baronet. The site dates from 1283 when Gloucester College was founded by Benedictine monks. Its position on the edge of eighteenth-century Oxford allowed it a unique luxury – the extensive gardens surrounding a lake that has become home to a variety of waterfowl. This is Diplock's daytime playground, through which he prowls at will and in which he lives up rather well to his name.

Blondie the duck regularly takes her ducklings to the college kitchens – a charming early springtime event that regrettably figures on Diplock's calendar. The resident grey squirrel population – though more adept at avoiding Diplock than waterfowl, is subject to the same arbitrary regime. Visitors and college residents alike are often startled by the sight and sound of Diplock streaking across the lawn in hot pursuit of a squirrel and scrambling determinedly up a sixty-foot tree.

One of Diplock's observation points

Left: On duck patrol

He hasn't had it entirely his own way with the squirrels, for there have been several stand-offs, culminating recently in a dash to the vet's with a howling Diplock. It says something for his spirit of determination that as soon as he was able, he resumed his high-altitiude squirrel patrol.

The author and publishers would like
to thank the following for their help and cooperation
in making this book possible:-

Dr B. A. Hepple and Mrs Mary Coussey, CLARE COLLEGE
Mr David Holton, FITZWILLIAM COLLEGE
Professor Peter Bayley, GONVILLE & CAIUS COLLEGE
Mr Peter Bacon, Angela Masters and Dr Mika Oldham, JESUS COLLEGE
Professor Patrick Bateson and Mrs Dusha Bateson, KING'S COLLEGE
Dr James Hickson, Sir Roger and Lady Margaret Tomkys, PEMBROKE COLLEGE
Sir Terence and Lady Ann English, ST CATHERINE'S COLLEGE
Revd George Bush, ST JOHN'S COLLEGE
Professor Anne Barton and Dr Hazel McLean, TRINITY COLLEGE
Dr Ivor Jones and Mr Ray James, WESLEY HOUSE
Philipa King, WESTCOTT HOUSE

Regius Professor of Divinity Keith Ward and Mrs Marian Ward, CHRIST CHURCH
Mrs Judith Mullee, HERTFORD COLLEGE
Dr Ian Archer, KEBLE COLLEGE
Mrs Anne Longshawe, LINACRE COLLEGE
Revd Dr E. W. Nicholson and family, ORIEL COLLEGE
Mrs Alison Beech, ST JOHN'S COLLEGE
Dr J. P. Barron and family, ST PETER'S COLLEGE
Heidi Carlton, WORCESTER COLLEGE

The line-drawing of Fitzwilliam College, Cambridge, by David Seber, is used by permission of the College.
The pen and ink drawing of Wesley House, Cambridge is used by permission of the artist, Alison Howell.
The pen and ink drawing of Westcott House, Cambridge is used by permission of the artist,
Andrew Parsons, now Vicar of Wroxham.
The line-drawing of Linacre College, Oxford is used by permission of the Principal and Fellows of the College.
The drawing of Keble College, Oxford, by William Butterfield, is used by permission of the
Warden and Fellows of the College.
The line-drawing of the Canal House, the Master's Lodgings at St Peter's College, Oxford, is used by
permission of the College.